My Useful Machines

Penelope Santos

Rosen
REAL
READERS

Rosen
Classroom™
New York

1

This is my uncle.

He works at a factory.

My uncle fixes machines.

He uses tools to fix machines.

Here are his tools.

Machines have parts.

My uncle fixes broken parts.

He replaces old parts.

Metal parts rust.

My uncle removes rusty screws.
He replaces them with new ones.

This is a lathe.

A lathe spins wood.

Someone shapes the wood
as it spins.

Gears help a lathe spin.

Gears are wheels with teeth.

They spin to make machines work.

Sometimes gears get stuck.

My uncle oils gears.

This helps them spin.

Some machines are run
by computers.
This woman controls machines
with a computer.

Sometimes computers break. Sometimes my uncle also fixes broken computers.

Words to Know

computer

gears

lathe

machine

rust

tools